CHRIST IS ALL

A STUDY ON THE BOOK OF COLOSSIANS

BY SARA BRANSTETTER

ISBN 9781731281999

AUTHOR: Sara Branstetter

LAYOUT: Jill E. McCormick

CONTENTS

Preface and Process   4

WEEK 1: Colossians 1:3-14   6
Epignosis of God's Will

WEEK 2: Colossians 1:15-23   22
Supremacy of Christ

WEEK 3: Colossians 1:24-29 and 2:1-5   41
Paul's Ministry: Our Ministry

WEEK 4: Colossians 2:6-15   66
Identity and Purpose

WEEK 5: Colossians 2:16-23   88
Look to the Substance, Not the Shadow

WEEK 6: Colossians 3:1-11   108
Seek and Set

WEEK 7: Colossians 3:12-17   128
Put On and Put In

WEEK 8: Colossians 3:18-25 and 4:1   150
Households in Christ

WEEK 9: Colossians 4:2-18 and Philemon 1   167
Walking in Wisdom Toward Outsiders

Final Video: Teaching Notes   187

PREFACE AND PROCESS

I am so pleased that you have decided to join me for the next 10 weeks as we examine the living Word of God together. This study was written with two primary goals in mind.

First, that students would develop an understanding of the message of the book of Colossians (which is exceedingly timely and appropriate for the culture and climate that we find ourselves in today) and second, that students would make progress in their habits of personal Scripture study.

According to 2 Timothy 3:16-17, "all Scripture is God-breathed and is useful for teaching, rebuking, correcting, and training in righteousness, so that the servant of God may be thoroughly equipped for every good work" (NIV). **All** Scripture, not just some or parts, but all of it. And it is imperative that we set our minds to seek first the kingdom of God in the written Word of the Bible so that we are thoroughly equipped for every good work. Jesus truly is the best teacher, but we must show up to class!

As we study Colossians, use this opportunity to not only grow in your knowledge and understanding of the text, but in the discipline of Scripture study itself. Below is a summary of the process I have been taught and use to study the Bible on my own. As you make your way through your daily homework, you will see evidence of this process in the writing.

1. Begin by praying. The study of Scripture is quite different than a cursory read through of the text of the Bible and we cannot expect to fully grasp what we are studying without appealing to our teacher, Jesus Christ, for help. Pray and ask the Lord to guide your study by clearing your mind of preconceived ideas and biases. Ask Him to illuminate the deep Truths of His Word to your heart.

2. Read the text in a few different translations. Read the text before and after the day's passage. Ensure you understand the context of the specific text you are studying. Ask questions of the text. What is the central theme or message? Why is the text included in the counsel of Scripture? What does it say about God, His plan, or His ways? What does it say about man or his relationship to God? Pray and ask the Lord to guide you to the answers to your questions.

3. Consider the words used in the Scripture passage. Why were the specific words chosen? Look up words in a dictionary or a Hebrew or Greek concordance. Look to see if the words used had a different connotation during the writing of the Bible than they do now. Find when and how the words are used elsewhere in the Bible.

4. Utilize commentaries from respected teachers and scholars. But always keep in mind that only the Bible is inerrant and authoritative.

5. Finally, look for a specific promise to trust in or a specific call to obedience to act on. Then thank the Lord for His loving-kindness that made His Word available to His people.

The study of Scripture is a wonderfully interactive discipline. As you set your mind to learn and engage, the Holy Spirit will meet you and you will quickly find that it becomes a sort of a living prayer – a dialogue back and forth with God. Don't be discouraged if it takes some time to develop this dialogue but trust that your perseverance won't be in vain. God is faithful. And don't be disappointed if there isn't a massive revelation of Truth dropped neatly into your lap every time you read and study. Trust the Lord for His timing for these kinds of experiences and know that in the meantime, He is building a foundation of Truth that will hold you steadfast for the rest of your life.

This study has accompanying teaching videos that can be accessed online by going to www.youtube.com and entering "Sara Branstetter" in the search box.

WEEK 1:
Epignosis of God's Will
COLOSSIANS 1:3-14

DAY ONE

Video Teaching Notes:

Listen to the entire book of Colossians on biblegateway.com or the YouVersion Bible app. Read Colossians 1:3-14 in two or three different translations (ESV, NIV, KJV, AMP).

1. Summarize Paul's central themes in this passage.

Col. 1's Consistent faith & love to others
Hungry for more

2. What excites you or captures your interest in this passage?

V. 8 - how thoroughly love worked into their lives by the Spirit

9 ask God to give us wise minds & spirits attuned to His will
as you learn how God works, you learn how to do your work

3. Are any parts of the passage difficult to understand? What questions do you have about the text?

DAY TWO

"We always thank God, the Father of our Lord Jesus Christ, when we pray for you, since we heard of your faith in Christ Jesus and of the love that you have for all the saints, because of the hope laid up for you in heaven. Of this you have Heard before in the word of the truth, the gospel, which has come to you..."
- Colossians 1:3-6a

1. What is the *hope* that Paul is referencing?

Eternal life

2. Look up the following Scriptures and describe how they better inform your understanding of this *hope*.

Acts 23:6 – *hope + resurrection of the dead*

1 Thessalonians 5:5-8 – *hope of salvation*

1 Timothy 1:1 – *Christ, our living hope*

Titus 2:11-13 – *looking for the blessed hope + appearing of Christ*

1 Peter 1:3-5 – *living hope future in heaven - starts now*

3. How does hope get *laid up* for us in Heaven?

4. Read verses 3-5 in the NIV. How does hope affect or influence faith and love in a believer?

Steadfastness

5. What are you hoping for right now? Were you to receive what is hoped for, would the result be an increase in faith in Jesus or love for the saints? Why or why not?

to do God's will

6. How did the gospel *come to* the Colossians?

learned from Epaphras

7. How does the gospel *come to* people today? Read Romans 10:13-15.

God sends persons to preach the Gospel

8. How did the gospel come to you? Do you find it easy or difficult to bring the gospel to others? Pray and ask the Lord for help in bringing the gospel to those around you.

DAY THREE

"...as indeed in the whole world it is bearing fruit and increasing - as it also does among you, since the day you heard it and understood the grace of God in truth, just as you learned it from Epaphras our beloved fellow servant. He is a faithful minister of Christ on your behalf and has made known to us your love in the Spirit."
- Colossians 1:6b-8

1. What kind of *fruit* does the gospel bear?

2. Read verse 6 in the AMP. The gospel "still is growing" today. What drives that growth according to the AMP?

3. What does this mean for us as we seek to preach the gospel? How do we labor rightly to spread the good news?

4. What if we fail to discharge our commission to preach the gospel? Will it fail or stop growing? Read Luke 19:28–40.

5. Paul writes to the Colossians that the gospel has been bearing fruit and increasing since the day that they heard the Word and "truly understood God's grace" (NIV). What happens when a person hears but does not understand?

6. How can you know when a person has both heard and understood? What results might you expect?

7. Read James 1:22–25 in the ESV. Is there anything in your own heart in which you know you have been a hearer, but not a doer? If so, what? Repent and ask the Lord to strengthen you to be a doer!

DAY FOUR

"And so, from the day we heard, we have not ceased to pray for you, asking that you may be filled with the knowledge of his will in all spiritual wisdom and understanding, so as to walk in a manner worthy of the Lord, fully pleasing to him: bearing fruit in every good work and increasing in the knowledge of God; being strengthened with all power, according to his glorious might, for all endurance and patience with joy."
- Colossians 1:9-11

1. Look up the following words in the dictionary and note their definitions.

Filled –

Knowledge –

Spiritual –

Wisdom –

Understanding –

2. Pulling from the definitions above, summarize what Paul is praying would happen in verse 9.

3. What fruit should follow this action? How do you know?

4. Read Ephesians 4:1-6. What manner of walk is worthy of the Lord?

5. Look up the word *walk* in the dictionary and note the definition below.

6. Why do you think Paul used the word *walk* here? What point was he trying to make?

7. Is there some respect of your walk which is not worthy of the Lord? What is it? How would a filling of the knowledge of God's will affect your ability to walk in a way that pleases God?

8. Verse 9 begins with Paul praying that the Colossians would be *filled with the knowledge of God's will.* Verse 10 ends with him praying that they might *increase in the knowledge of God.* How might being filled with a knowledge of God's will translate to knowing God?

9. Paul prays that the Colossians would be *strengthened with all power*. Look up the verses below and note how the power described can strengthen a believer.

Acts 1:8 –

Romans 1:16 –

1 Corinthians 6:14 –

Ephesians 3:16-17 –

2 Peter 1:3 –

10. How does this power make it so that you "may have great endurance and patience" (NIV)? What do you need endurance and patience for right now? Pray that you would be strengthened with God's power for this.

DAY FIVE

"...giving thanks to the Father, who has qualified you to share in the inheritance of the saints in light. He has delivered us from the domain of darkness and transferred us to the kingdom of his beloved Son, in whom we have redemption, the forgiveness of sins."
- Colossians 1:12-14

1. Look up the word *qualified* in the dictionary and note the definition below.

2. How has the Father *qualified* you?

3. Look up the following Scriptures and note how they inform your understanding of your inheritance.

Psalm 16:5-6 -

Isaiah 54:17 -

Matthew 25:34-36 -

Ephesians 1:11-14 -

1 Peter 1:3-5 -

4. Read Revelation 21:1-4. What do you have to look forward to inheriting?

5. How do Deuteronomy 32:9 and 1 Kings 8:50-53 (NIV) affect your understanding of your inheritance?

6. What is the *domain of darkness*?

7. *Transferred* means to remove from one place to another. You have been removed from the domain of darkness and *transferred to the kingdom of God's beloved Son*. Make a list of everything you know about the kingdom of God's Son. For help, search for the keyword *kingdom* in a Bible concordance either online or in the back of your Bible. Pay close attention to references found in Matthew, Mark, Luke, and John.

8. Re-read Colossians 1:3–14. Paraphrase the passage in just a few sentences.

9. How is this message relevant to you or your context today?

WEEK 2:

Supremacy of Christ

COLOSSIANS 1:15-23

DAY ONE

Video Teaching Notes:

Listen to the entire book of Colossians on www.biblegateway.com or the YouVersion Bible app. Read Colossians 1:15-23 in two or three different translations (ESV, NIV, KJV, AMP).

1. Summarize Paul's central themes in this passage.

2. What excites you or captures your interest in this passage?

3. Are any parts of the passage difficult to understand? What questions do you have about the text?

DAY TWO

"He is the image of the invisible God, the firstborn of all creation. For by him all things were created, in heaven and on earth, visible and invisible, whether thrones or dominions or rulers or authorities — all things were created through him and for him."
- Colossians 1:15-16

1. Look up the following words in the dictionary and note their definitions below.

Image –

Invisible –

2. Read Colossians 1:15 in the AMP. How does this translation affect your understanding of the passage?

3. Read John 1:18 in the NIV. What information, experience, or blessing has Jesus made available to you?

4. Read Hebrews 1:3. How do you understand what it is for Jesus to be the *image* of God in this passage?

5. Look up *firstborn* in the dictionary and note the definition below.

6. What does it mean that Jesus is the *firstborn of all creation*?

7. Was Jesus created? How do you know?

8. Read Psalm 89:19-29. Who is this Psalm about and how is he described in verse 27?

9. Was David the firstborn among his brothers? See 1 Samuel 16:1-13.

10. Based on the information about David, now what do you think is meant by firstborn in Colossians 1:15?

11. How many times does Paul use the word *all* in verse 16? Why do you think this is?

12. What does it mean that all things were created:

– by Him?

– through Him?

– for Him?

13. Read John 1:3. Was anything created or made apart from Jesus? Does this include Satan and his followers?

14. Which is superior – Creator or created? Why? See Psalm 102:25-27.

15. How might you better utilize your resources for Jesus? Are there any resources, people, or possessions that you need to set apart to Christ? If so, pray now and commit them to the firstborn of all creation for whom these things were created.

DAY THREE

"And he is before all things, and in him all things hold together. And he is the head of the body, the church. He is the beginning, the firstborn from the dead, that in everything he might be preeminent."
-Colossians 1:17-18

1. Look up John 1:1 and John 8:58. What do these passages indicate about Jesus?

2. What does Paul mean when he says in him all things hold together? Can you give some examples?

3. The AMP renders the words "hold together" as "consist" or "cohere." Does this change or enhance your understanding of how all things hold together in Christ? How so?

4. Why does Paul call the church a body? See Romans 12:4-5.

5. What are the physical functions of a head?

6. What happens to a body when it is separated from its head?

7. According to Ephesians 1:22-23, what is Jesus's role in the body and what is the church's role in the body?

8. What happens when both Jesus and the church fulfill their roles? See Ephesians 4:15–16.

9. Paul calls Jesus the *beginning* and the *firstborn from the dead*. What is he trying to communicate in juxtaposing these truths about Jesus?

10. Based on your study of the word *firstborn* on day 2, what does it mean that Jesus is the *firstborn from the dead*?

11. Look up the word *preeminence* and note the definition below.

12. Read verse 18 in the NIV. What word is used instead of preeminence? Look up the new word in the dictionary and note its definition below.

13. Why does Paul spend so much time emphasizing Christ's supremacy? What is he ultimately trying to communicate to his readers?

14. How does Christ's preeminence personally affect, influence, or touch you? Do you view it as positive or negative? Why?

DAY FOUR

"For in him all the fullness of God was pleased to dwell,
and through him to reconcile to himself all things,
whether on earth or in heaven, making peace
by the blood of his cross."
- Colossians 1:19-20

1. According to verse 19, all the fullness of God dwelled in Jesus. Look up the Scriptures below and note what they teach us about Father God.

Deuteronomy 32:6 –

Psalm 86:5 –

Isaiah 6:2-3 –

Isaiah 44:24 –

1 Corinthians 1:9 –

1 John 4:7-8 –

2. Were all these attributes of Father God found in Christ? Yes or no? How do you know?

3. What does it mean that the fullness of God *was pleased* to dwell in Christ? Why do you think Paul mentioned the Father's pleasure here? What does it signify or convey?

4. Look up the word *reconcile* in the dictionary and note the definition below.

5. Reconciliation implies prior conflict. What is this conflict? See Ephesians 2:1-3.

6. The conflict affected *all things*, according to Colossians 1:20. Read Genesis 3:14–19 and note what was affected by this conflict.

7. Was anything unaffected by this conflict? If so, what was it?

8. Read Leviticus 17:11 in the NIV. How does the blood make peace (atone)?

9. Read 2 Corinthians 5:17–21. How did God accomplish this reconciliation?

10. The Greek word for *peace* in Colossians 1:20 means "to go away or to go slowly away, to depart, withdraw oneself, with the idea of going without noise or notice."[1] What does this mean for you personally? Do you experience Christ's peace in your life? Why or why not?

1 Strong, James. "Peace." The New Strong's Expanded Exhaustive Concordance of the Bible Red Letter Edition, Thomas Nelson Publishers, 2001, pp 78.

DAY FIVE

"And you, who once were alienated and hostile in mind,
doing evil deeds, he has now reconciled in his body of
flesh by his death, in order to present you holy and
blameless and above reproach before him, if indeed
you continue in the faith, stable and steadfast,
not shifting from the hope of the gospel
that you heard, which has been proclaimed
in all creation under heaven, and of which
I, Paul, became a minister."
-Colossians 1:21-23

1. Read verse 21 in the KJV. How is it different from the ESV?

2. In what three ways were you once alienated from God?

Romans 5:10 –

Ephesians 2:12 –

Ephesians 4:18 –

3. Read Romans 7:4 and 2 Corinthians 5:21. What was God's purpose in this act of reconciliation?

4. Who are you being *presented to*?

5. Look up the following words in the dictionary and make note of their definitions.

Holy –

Blameless –

Above Reproach –

6. Paul sets off verse 23 with the word *if.* Is he qualifying or putting a condition on his statement in verse 22? What is Paul saying or suggesting?

7. Verse 23 utilizes architectural terms – *stable, steadfast, not shifting.* Why did Paul choose to use these specific words in this message?

8. What is the *hope of the gospel*?

9. In your own words, summarize verses 21-23.

10. Re-read Colossians 1:15-23. Paraphrase the passage in just a few sentences.

11. How is this message relevant to you or your context today?

WEEK 3:
Paul's Ministry: Our Ministry
COLOSSIANS 1:24-29 AND 2:1-5

DAY ONE

Video Teaching Notes:

Listen to the entire book of Colossians on
www.biblegateway.com or the YouVersion Bible app.
Read Colossians 1:24-29 and 2:1-5 in two or three different
translations (ESV, NIV, KJV, AMP).

1. Summarize Paul's central themes in this passage.

2. What excites you or captures your interest in this
passage?

3. Are any parts of the passage difficult to
understand? What questions do you have about the text?

DAY TWO

"Now I rejoice in my sufferings for your sake, and in my flesh I am filling up what is lacking in Christ's afflictions for the sake of his body, that is, the church, of which I became a minister according to the stewardship from God that was given to me for you, to make the word of God fully known, the mystery hidden for ages and generations but now revealed to his saints. To them God chose to make known how great among the Gentiles are the riches of the glory of this mystery, which is Christ in you, the hope of glory."
- Colossians 1:24-27

1. What were some of Paul's sufferings? Read the following Scriptures and make a list.

- 2 Corinthians 6:3-10
- 2 Corinthians 11:23-29

2. Given the intensity, duration, and types of suffering that Paul had endured, how was he able to *rejoice* in it and through it? What was Paul's hope? See Romans 5:1-5, James 1:2-4, and 1 Peter 4:14-16 for help.

3. Romans 12:2 states, "Do not conform to the pattern of this world, but be transformed by the renewing of your mind. Then you will be able to test and approve what God's will is – his good, pleasing and perfect will" (NIV). What is the "pattern of this world" with regard to suffering? What is God's will regarding suffering? What is one way you can renew your mind today so that when faced with suffering, you may rejoice as Paul did?

4. What is meant by "I am filling up what is lacking in Christ's afflictions"? What might this indicate regarding Jesus's work on the cross? Was it enough? Why or why not?

5. The Greek word for filling up means "to fill up in turn or undertake to a part or share."[2] Is this part or share just for Paul? See 2 Timothy 1:8 in the NIV.

6. According to the letter to the Colossians, who benefits from Paul's sufferings?

2 Strong, James. "Fill." The New Strong's Expanded Exhaustive Concordance of the Bible Red Letter Edition, Thomas Nelson Publishers, 2001, pp 29.

7. Can you give other examples from Scripture of how suffering has benefited the church?

8. Does the church continue to benefit from the sufferings of its people? Why or why not?

9. Read verse 25 in the NIV. How does it differ from the ESV? What was Paul's job?

10. What is the *mystery* Paul references in verse 26? Why did he choose to use this word?

11. Who is *them* in verse 27?

12. Who are the saints of God? See 1 Corinthians 1:2 in the KJV.

13. Read Romans 1:16 in the NIV. Who receives salvation first? Through whom did the message of salvation to the Jews come?

14. Read Hebrews 6:19–20. How does this passage better inform your understanding of Colossians 1:27?

15. Consider the phrase *Christ in you, the hope of glory*. What do you understand this to mean? Does it personally impact you? Why or why not?

DAY THREE

"Him we proclaim, warning everyone and teaching everyone with all wisdom, that we may present everyone mature in Christ. For this I toil, struggling with all his energy that he powerfully works within me."
- Colossians 1:28-29

1. Read verse 28 in the KJV. How many times does Paul use the words "every man"? Why does he do this?

2. Look up the word warn in the dictionary and note the definition below.

3. What was Paul warning every man of?

4. What should we warn others of today?

5. Look up the word teach in the dictionary and note the definition below.

6. What was Paul trying to teach every man?

7. What should we teach others today?

8. What provisions has God made to teach us? Look up each Scripture below and indicate what God uses to teach His people.

Jeremiah 3:15 –

John 16:13 –

2 Timothy 3:16–17 –

9. What is Paul trying to achieve in proclaiming, warning, and teaching?

10. What are some differences between warning and teaching? Why is it important to utilize both strategies in ministry?

11. What does it mean to be mature in Christ? See Ephesians 5:27 and 1 John 2:12-14.

12. Ask the Lord for one step you can take today toward maturity in Christ and wait for His answer. Record it below.

13. Read verses 28-29 in the NIV. To what end or goal was Paul working?

14. How does Paul describe the manner in which he works? See a few different translations for descriptions.

15. What was God's provision for Paul so that he could sustain this type of work?

16. Read 1 Corinthians 15:10. What exactly is at work within a believer who labors for Christ?

17. Do you feel weary by working for Jesus? If so, are you drawing from the well of grace or the well of your own strength? How can you turn from the wrong well to the right one? See Matthew 11:28-30 in the ESV. What is one step you can take today to labor by the grace of God?

DAY FOUR

"For I want you to know how great a struggle I have for you and for those at Laodicea and for all who have not seen me face to face, that their hearts may be encouraged, being knit together in love, to reach all the riches of full assurance of understanding and the knowledge of God's mystery, which is Christ, in whom are hidden all the treasures of wisdom and knowledge."
- Colossians 2:1-3

1. Paul states in verse 1 that he is having a struggle for the Colossians, Laodiceans, and any who *have not seen him face to face*. The Greek word for struggle (or conflict in the KJV) is the same word used to describe the assembly of the Olympics or the Greek National Games.[3] What is Paul communicating in comparing his feelings to a major sporting event?

3 Strong, James. "Conflict." The New Strong's Expanded Exhaustive Concordance of the Bible Red Letter Edition, Thomas Nelson Publishers, 2001, pp 5.

2. Have you ever *struggled* on behalf of someone you have not seen face to face? What form did your struggle take?

3. Read verse 2 in the NIV. Paul starts with two goals in mind for the believers at Colossae. What are they?

    1.

    2.

4. These are precursors to Paul's next goal. If believers are "encouraged in heart and united in love" (NIV), what should result, according to verse 2? Notice the words "so that" for a clue.

5. What does Paul mean by "the full riches of complete understanding" (NIV)? See the AMP for help.

6. How might encouragement of heart and unity in love lead to these riches of understanding?

7. Read Proverbs 3:5-6. What are you instructed **not** to do?

8. According to the NIV, seeing believers reach the "full riches of complete understanding" isn't Paul's end game. What is? Notice the words "in order that" for a clue.

9. When we know the mystery of God, "namely, Christ" (NIV), what do we have access to, according to verse 3?

10. How does Paul's message directly contradict the message of the Gnostics? Can wisdom or knowledge be found apart from the Lord? Why or why not?

11. Consider your heart, do you lack encouragement, comfort, or unity in love with other believers?

12. How might this be robbing you of greater things in Christ?

13. Have you tried to attain to the riches of full assurance without the precursors?

14. Pray and ask the Lord to show you how you might walk in encouragement of heart or greater unity in love.

DAY FIVE

"I say this in order that no one may delude you with plausible arguments. For though I am absent in body, yet I am with you in spirit, rejoicing to see your good order and the firmness of your faith in Christ."
- Colossians 2:4-5

1. Paul did not want the believers at Colossae to be deluded (deceived, misled, cheated, beguiled) by *plausible arguments*. Sum up what he says in Colossians 2:1-3 that might keep believers safe from this.

2. Look up the word *plausible* in the dictionary and note the definition below.

3. Read 2 Timothy 3:1–5. What is often the basis for a *plausible argument*? Pay close attention to verse 5.

4. Give an example of what it looks like to have an *appearance of godliness, but denying its power.* What does this mean?

5. What can happen to a believer who is misled by *plausible arguments*? See Ephesians 4:14 and 1 Timothy 4:1.

6. Is Paul's message relevant today? Why are *plausible arguments* so dangerous? What do we, as believers, stand to lose if we are misled or deceived?

7. How are we to judge if a *plausible argument* is true or false? Look up the Scriptures below and note what advice, caution, or help is offered.

Matthew 7:15-20 –

John 16:13 –

1 Thessalonians 5:20-22 –

1 John 4:1-3 –

8. Did Paul use *plausible arguments* or persuasive speech in sharing the gospel? See 1 Corinthians 2:1–5.

9. If not his speech, what made his arguments influential or authoritative? See also 1 Thessalonians 1:5.

10. How can we protect ourselves today from the deceit of *plausible arguments*?

11. Have you ever used deceitful or manipulative speech to convince people to turn to Christ? If so, repent now and ask the Lord to demonstrate His power in your message.

12. Read Colossians 2:5 in the AMP. What imagery is used to describe the good order of the Colossians? How does this better inform your understanding of how a church or body of believers should function?

13. Have you ever rejoiced or "joyed" (KJV) in the steadfastness of another believer? Who and why? Pray and thank the Lord now for those who stand firm in Christ around the world.

14. Re-read Colossians 1:24-29 and 2:1-5. Paraphrase the passage in just a few sentences.

15. How is this message relevant to you or your context today?

Identity and Purpose

COLOSSIANS 2:6-15

DAY ONE

Video Teaching Notes

Listen to the entire book of Colossians on www.biblegateway.com or the YouVersion Bible app. Read Colossians 2:6-15 in two or three different translations (ESV, NIV, KJV, AMP)."
-Colossians 1:21-23

1. Summarize Paul's central themes in this passage.

2. What excites you or captures your interest in this passage?

3. Are any parts of the passage difficult to understand? What questions do you have about the text?

DAY TWO

"Therefore, as you received Christ Jesus the Lord, so walk
in him, rooted and built up in him and established
in the faith, just as you were taught,
abounding in thanksgiving."
- Colossians 2:6-7

1. Read verse 6 in the NIV. How does it differ from the
ESV?

2. Why would Paul admonish believers to continue to
live their lives in Christ? Is it possible to not continue
to live this way? See Mark 4:1-20. What happens to the
seed that falls on rocky ground?

3. How do we *walk in Christ*? Look up the Scriptures below and note what they suggest.

John 14:21 –

Ephesians 5:1-2 –

1 John 2:6 –

4. Look up the word *rooted* in the dictionary and note the definition below.

5. Look up Jeremiah 17:7-8. What does a tree that is *rooted* in the Lord look like?

6. Read Revelation 22:16. What does Jesus refer to Himself as? What does this mean?

7. Look up the word *built* in the dictionary and note the definition below.

8. Based on this definition, what does it mean to be *built up in him*?

9. Can we build ourselves up apart from Christ? How do we do this? What happens when we do? See Luke 6:46–49.

10. Look up *established* in the dictionary and note the definition below.

11. What does it mean to be *established in the faith*?

12. Read Hebrews 11:8–13. What evidence do you see of how Abraham was *established in the faith*?

13. Look up the word *abounding* in the dictionary and note the definition below.

14. Look back over Colossians 1:3 through Colossians 2:7. How many times does Paul mention thankfulness (thanks, thanksgiving)? Why the repetition of this principal – what is Paul trying to communicate?

15. Do you abound in thanksgiving? Why or why not?

16. Spend 5 minutes making a list of everything you are thankful for.

17. Then pray and thank God for His abundant provision, mercy, and grace for you.

DAY THREE

"See to it that no one takes you captive by philosophy and empty deceit, according to human tradition, according to the elemental spirits of the world, and not according to Christ. For in him the whole fullness of deity dwells bodily, and you have been filled in him, who is the head of all rule and authority."
- Colossians 2:8-10

1. Begin by reading verse 8 in the KJV. What word does the passage start with?

2. Go to www.studylight.org.
- Click on Original Language Tools.
- In the Interlinear Search box, type in "Colossians 2:8" and click Go.
- Then, change the translation in the search box to the King James Version and click Search.
- Scroll down to the verse and hover your mouse over the word "Beware."
- When it highlights, click on it.
- The Thayer's/Strong's definitions will then load below the Scripture.
- Read the definition of "beware" and note it below.

3. Given this definition, what is Paul suggesting the believers do?

4. The KJV renders the word "captive" as "spoil." Paul is warning his readers to be on guard against being carried off as spoils. What does this mean?

5. Directly translated from the Greek, "philosophy" means "love of wisdom."[4] What was wrong with the kind of wisdom Paul was speaking of?

4 "Philosophy." Strong's Edition: King James Version, updated ed. StudyLight.org, https://www.studylight.org/interlinear-bible/colossians.

6. What kinds of *human traditions* did Paul speak of? How do you know?

7. What is wrong with the wisdom associated with *human tradition*? See Matthew 15:1-9.

8. What are elemental *spirits of the world*? Look up the Scriptures below and note what information you can derive from them regarding the *elemental spirits of the world.*

Galatians 4:3, 9 –

2 Peter 3:10, 12 –

9. Can you name some *human traditions* or *elemental spirits of the world* that have the power to carry you off as spoils today? What should you be on guard against?

10. Is there a philosophy *according to Christ*? Where do you find it?

11. What kind of fruit does the philosophy that is *according to human tradition* bear? What kind of fruit does the philosophy that is *according to Christ* bear? See James 3:13-18

12. Why would Paul turn his discourse from captivity by philosophy to the fullness of Christ? What is he arguing in this?

13. Read verses 9 and 10 in the KJV. What word is used instead of filled in verse 10?

14. Does this change your answer to question 12? Why or why not?

15. Conclude today's study by reading Proverbs 8. Does the Lord value wisdom? Pray and ask the Lord to increase your understanding and to stoke the fires of love and desire for wisdom within your heart.

DAY FOUR

"In him also you were circumcised with a circumcision
made without hands, by putting off the body of
the flesh, by the circumcision of Christ, having
been buried with him in baptism, in which you
were also raised with him through faith in
the powerful working of God, who raised
him from the dead."
- Colossians 2:11-12

1. Read Genesis 17:9-14. What was the purpose of circumcision in the Old Testament?

2. While circumcision was largely seen as an outward sign of the covenant between God and Israel, the Lord intended an inward change associated with it. What was intended? See Deuteronomy 30:1-6.

3. Did the Jews remain faithful to their covenant, outward and inward? See Jeremiah 4:1-4.

4. According to the Scriptures you have just read, what was God's priority for His people, Israel? Did physical circumcision accomplish it?

5. Read Romans 2:25-29. Where does the value in circumcision lie? Who is responsible for doing the circumcising?

6. Is circumcision still required to be in covenant with God? How do we now enter into covenant with God? See Galatians 3:23-29.

7. Read Colossians 2:11-12 in the NIV. According to verse 11, what was "put off" when you were circumcised by Christ?

8. What are the implications of this?

9. Do you still struggle with a *stubborn* (Deuteronomy 10:16) or wayward heart? In what specific area(s) is your heart stubborn? Pray and ask the Lord to help you walk in your identity as Abraham's heir and not as one who is "excluded from citizenship in Israel and foreigners to the covenants of the promise, without hope and without God in the world" (Ephesians 2:12 NIV).

10. Read Romans 6:3-7. What does Paul mean by his use of the word *united* (united with him in a death like his or united with him in a resurrection like his) in verse 5?

11. If you have been united with Christ in His baptism and resurrection, through faith in the working of God, does anything else need to be done to accomplish your circumcision or bring you to fullness in Christ? Why or why not?

DAY FIVE

"And you, who were dead in your trespasses and the uncircumcision of your flesh, God made alive together with him, having forgiven us all our trespasses, by canceling the record of debt that stood against us with its legal demands. This he set aside, nailing it to the cross. He disarmed the rulers and authorities and put them to open shame, by triumphing over them in him."
- Colossians 2:13-15

1. Verses 13-15 are a succinct presentation of the gospel. Summarize them in your own words.

2. How were you once "dead in your trespasses or sins" (KJV)? Read Ephesians 2:1-3.

3. What does Paul mean in verse 13 by saying God made you *alive together with him*? What does the word "with" denote? Look back at Day 4 questions 10 and 11.

4. According to verses 13 and 14, how does God forgive us *all our trespasses*?

5. What is the *record of debt that stood against us*?

6. Read verse 14 in the KJV. Then go to
www.studylight.org.

- Click on Original Language Tools.
- In the Interlinear Search box, type in "Colossians 2:14" and click Go.
- Then change the translation in the search box to the King James Version and click Search.
- Scroll down to the verse and hover your mouse over the word "handwriting."
- When it highlights, click on it. The Thayer's/Strong's definitions will then load below the Scripture.
- Repeat with the word "ordinances."

Read the definitions of each word and note what they suggest about the *record of debt*. What imagery was Paul using to help his readers understand the message of the gospel?

7. Look up the Lord's prayer in Matthew 6:9-13. Read it in the New Living Translation (NLT) and the (ESV). How do the translations differ in verse 12? What specific words are used in each translation to describe what must be forgiven?

8. With your answer to question 7 in mind, read Romans 6:23. What are the *legal demands* of our debt?

9. What does God do with our record of debt? Look up the word "blotting" (KJV) in the dictionary and note the definition below. What does it mean that our debt was blotted out or cancelled?

10. Who are the *rulers and authorities* spoken of inverse 15? See Ephesians 6:12.

11. According to 1 John 3:8, why did the Son of God appear?

12. In His disarming of rulers and authorities, does Jesus accomplish the task for which He appeared in question 11? How so?

13. What are the practical implications for you of Jesus's disarming of and triumphing over rulers and authorities?

14. Re-read Colossians 2:6–15. Paraphrase the passage in just a few sentences.

15. How is this message relevant to you or your context today?

Look to the Substance, Not the Shadow

COLOSSIANS 2:16-23

DAY ONE

Video Teaching Notes

Listen to the entire book of Colossians on www.biblegateway.com or the YouVersion Bible app. Read Colossians 2:16-23 in two or three different translations (ESV, NIV, KJV, AMP).

1. Summarize Paul's central themes in this passage.

2. What excites you or captures your interest in this passage?

3. Are any parts of the passage difficult to understand? What questions do you have about the text?

DAY TWO

"Therefore let no one pass judgment on you in questions of food and drink, or with regard to a festival or a new moon or a Sabbath. These are a shadow of the things to come, but the substance belongs to Christ."
- Colossians 2:16-17

1. Paul begins this section of Colossians with the word *therefore*. This word links the previous passage to his instruction to *let no one pass judgment on you*. How do his writings in last week's study inform or affect what he has to say beginning in verse 16? What does it mean to *let no one pass judgment on you*?

2. What is Paul talking about with regard to *food and drink, a festival, a new moon, or a Sabbath*? Where did these customs come from and who practiced them? Look up the Scriptures below and write down what information they have to offer about these practices.

Deuteronomy 14:1–21 –

Leviticus 23 –

1 Chronicles 23:1–5, 28–32 –

Ezekiel 45:16–17 –

3. Based on your understanding of these practices, who might have been trying to pass judgement on the Colossians? What message might they have been teaching to the Colossians that Paul wanted to correct?

4. Read today's passage in the KJV. What word is used instead of substance?

5. The "body" is that which casts the shadow, not the shadow itself. On the table below, make a list of the properties of a shadow and a body (or the "reality," according to the NIV). How are they alike or different?

The Shadow	The Body

6. Read Hebrews 10:1. Why is the reality better than the shadow? What does it accomplish for us?

7. If the substance is found in the body of Christ, how then should we live? How does understanding this give us what we need to not let anyone judge us?

8. Read Romans 14. How should we conduct ourselves if we disagree about the rightness or holiness of certain practices (that aren't inherently sinful) such as what types of food to eat or what days to celebrate?

9. Romans 14:17 reads "For the kingdom of God is not a matter of eating and drinking, but of righteousness, peace, and joy in the Holy Spirit" (NIV). How might this understanding keep us from passing judgment on one another?

10. How have you let people judge you in the past? Were you able to stop it? Why or why not?

11. How can you avoid this in the future? Pray and ask the Lord to give you His truth to guard you from the earthly opinions of others. What is the mind of Christ (the thoughts, feelings, and purposes of His heart) regarding not letting anyone "act as your judge" (NASB) or "condemn you" (NLT)?

DAY THREE

"Let no one disqualify you, insisting on asceticism and worship of angels, going on in detail about visions, puffed up without reason by his sensuous mind, and not holding fast to the Head, from whom the whole body, nourished and knit together through its joints and ligaments, grows with a growth that is from God."
- Colossians 2:18-19

1. Look up the word *disqualify* and note the definition below.

2. Read verse 18 in the KJV. Then go to www.studylight.org.

- Click on Original Language Tools.
- In the Interlinear Search box, type in "Colossians 2:18" and click Go.
- Then, change the translation in the search box to the King James Version and click Search.
- Scroll down to the verse and hover your mouse over the word "beguile."
- When it highlights, click on it. The Thayer's/Strong's definitions will then load below the Scripture.

What is the definition of *beguile*? What imagery was Paul using to help his readers understand his message?

3. In sports terms, what might cause an umpire to disqualify a player?

4. Rewrite Paul's statement let no one disqualify you in your own words.

5. Paul notes 5 characteristics of those who were trying to disqualify or beguile the Colossians. Consider each idea, argument, or characteristic, and note the potential danger it presents.

CHARACTERISTIC	DEFINITION	DANGER
Insistence on asceticism or false humility (NIV)		
Worship of angels		
Going on about visions or intruding into those things which have not been seen (KJV)		
Puffed up without reason		
Not holding fast to the Head		

6. What is Paul suggesting will keep you from letting others disqualify you? How so?

7. Do you see these same characteristics in people today? Have you ever been beguiled by someone who demonstrates one or more of these traits? How were you freed from this?

8. Pray and ask the Lord to speak to your heart and show you if you are currently letting others disqualify you. What is one truth He can speak to you as one whom He has called qualified (Colossians 1:12)? Declare it now.

9. Read today's passage in the NIV. How is verse 19 different from the ESV?

10. Look back at the study for week 2, day 3. What did you note happens to a body when it is separated from (or loses connection with) its head? What had happened to those (the Gnostics) who were trying to persuade the Colossians to follow their beliefs?

11. What or who is the "body" referenced in verse 19? How does the body get nourished or ministered to (KJV)?

12. What does "grows with a growth that is from God" (Col. 2:19) mean? How is this possible?

13. Do you personally see growth in your life that is from God? How do you know it's from God? Is there anything impeding that growth? Ask the Lord to show you any weed or lack in nourishment that might be impeding your growth in the body. How might the impediment be removed?

DAY FOUR

"If with Christ you died to the elemental spirits of the world, why, as if you were still alive in the world, do you submit to regulations – "Do not handle, Do not taste, Do not touch" (referring to things that all perish as they are used)—according to human precepts and teachings?"
-Colossians 2:20-22

1. Look back at week 4, day 3. What are the *elemental spirits of the world*?

2. What does it benefit you *if with Christ you died*? How did you die with Christ? Read Romans 6:1-10 and Galatians 2:20.

3. What does it mean to be *alive in the world* or to "belong to the world" (NIV)?

4. What happens to those who *submit to regulations according to human precepts and teachings* or *turn back* (Galatians 4:9)? Read Galatians 4:8–11 and note what it suggests.

5. What does it mean that these things (regulations according to human precepts and teachings) will *perish as they are used*? Are there precepts and teachings which do not perish? Read 1 Peter 1:22–25. What does this suggest for you?

6. Look up Isaiah 29:13 in the NIV. What does the Lord desire from those who worship Him?

7. Ultimately, what is the purpose of Paul's question posed in verses 20-22?

8. Are there aspects of your life in which you live as though you are still *alive in the world*? Ask the Lord what part of your nature does this type of living appeal to. Does He offer you a better or more satisfactory way? What is it? Moving forward, how can you live as one who is dead to the elemental spirits of the world?

DAY FIVE

"These have indeed an appearance of wisdom in promoting self-made religion and asceticism and severity to the body, but they are of no value in stopping the indulgence of the flesh."
- Colossians 2:23

1. What are "these" at the beginning of verse 23?

2. Look up the word appearance in the dictionary and note the definition below.

3. Read Colossians 2:23 in the NIV. What about "self-imposed worship" has an appearance of wisdom? Why is it only an appearance? What is the reality of wisdom with regard to worship? See Chronicles 16:25-29.

4. What about "false humility" (NIV) has an appearance of wisdom? Why is it only an appearance? What is the reality of wisdom with regard to humility? See Proverbs 15:33 and 22:4.

5. What about "harsh treatment of the body" (NIV) has an appearance of wisdom? Why is it only an appearance? What is the reality with regard to treatment of the body? See Romans 12:1 and 1 Corinthians 6:13, 19–20.

6. Look up 1 Corinthians 9:24–27. Does this writing, also by the apostle Paul, contradict his words in his letter to the Colossians? Why or why not?

7. What, then, is the purpose of striking a blow to our bodies in order to bring them into "subjection" (KJV)?

8. Look up the word *indulgence* in the dictionary and note the definition below.

9. What is the *indulgence of the flesh*? See Romans 8:5-6 and Galatians 5:16-17.

10. If these things (self-made religion, asceticism, and severity to the body) do not have any value in stopping the indulgence of the flesh, then what does? Read Luke 9:23-25, 1 Timothy 4:8, and Hebrews 13:9.

11. Are you indulging your flesh by any of your beliefs or practices? Ask the Lord to show you any hidden sin in your heart. What is His truth about these beliefs or practices and how might you turn from the shadow to the reality?

12. Re-read Colossians 2:16–23. Paraphrase the passage in just a few sentences.

13. How is this message relevant to you or your context today?

WEEK 6:
Seek and Set
COLOSSIANS 3:1-11

DAY ONE

Video Teaching Notes

Listen to the entire book of Colossians on www.biblegateway.com or the YouVersion Bible app. Read Colossians 3:1-11 in two or three different translations (ESV, NIV, KJV, AMP).

1. Summarize Paul's central themes in this passage.

2. What excites you or captures your interest in this passage?

3. Are any parts of the passage difficult to understand? What questions do you have about the text?

DAY TWO

"If then you have been raised with Christ, seek the things that are above, where Christ is, seated at the right hand of God. Set your minds on things that are above, not on things that are on earth. For you have died, and your life is hidden with Christ in God. When Christ who is your life appears, then you also will appear with him in glory."
- Colossians 3:1-4

1. What does it mean to have *been raised with Christ*? To raise implies that at one point, an object was lowered, lying down, or depressed. What were you lifted from? See Romans 6:9–11.

2. What are *the things that are above*? Give examples. See 1 Chronicles 22:19, 2 Corinthians 4:18, and Philippians 4:8.

3. What are *things that are on earth*? Give examples.
See 1 John 2:15-17.

4. Read Matthew 6:33 and 7:7. Seek means to covet
earnestly or strive after. How do you *seek the things
that are above?*

5. How do you *set your mind* on something? Read verse
2 in the KJV. What word is used instead of "mind"?

6. In the Greek, *set your mind* can rendered "be minded in a certain way." [5] Can we accomplish this ourselves? How can we be *minded* about the things above? See Romans 12:2.

7. The verb "set" implies both a present and an ongoing "setting" of the mind. Why is this necessary? Can you simply set the mind once and trust it to remain steadfast? Why or why not?

8. What is ultimately the fate of those whose minds are set on earthly things? See Philippians 3:18-19.

5 Strong, James. "Set." The New Strong's Expanded Exhaustive Concordance of the Bible Red Letter Edition, Thomas Nelson Publishers, 2001, pp 266.

9. How is your life *hidden with Christ in God*? What does this mean? What benefits does *hiddenness* afford you?

10. What is meant by *Christ who is your life*? See John 11:25.

11. How will your appearing with Christ in glory affect your earthly body? See Philippians 3:20-21 and 1 John 3:2.

12. What does Christ's appearing, as it is mentioned in Colossians 3:4, have to do with verses 1-3?

13. Ask the Lord to show you any of the ways you have set your mind on earthly things. What counterfeits are being offered in these earthly thoughts?

14. What is the truth that is available to you in the heavenly or "above" thoughts?

15. How could you experience satisfaction in setting your mind on things above?

DAY THREE

"Put to death therefore what is earthly in you: sexual immorality, impurity, passion, evil desire, and covetousness, which is idolatry. On account of these the wrath of God is coming."
- Colossians 3:5-6

1. Read today's passage in the KJV. What word is used instead of *put to death*? What are some synonyms for this word? What is Paul's intent in using such strong language?

2. Based on verses 1-4 from yesterday's study, why should we put things to death?

3. Yesterday, in verse 2, you read Paul's warning to not set your mind on things that are on earth. In verse 5 of today's passage, he takes it a step farther and says to kill what is earthly in you. How are these two things – the mind and the behaviors – related? How do they influence one another?

4. Read the definitions[6] below and note what these *earthly* things have in common. See verse 6.

a. Sexual Immorality – Illicit sexual appetites or behaviors

b. Impurity – Uncleanliness or lustful uncleanliness associated with luxurious or loose living

c. Passion – Depravity or vileness

d. Evil Desire – Evil or base cravings or longings for what is forbidden

e. Covetousness – Greedy desire to have more

6 "Colossians 3:5." Strong's Edition: King James Version, updated ed. StudyLight.org, https://www.studylight.org/interlinear-bible/colossians.

5. Look up the word *idolatry* in the dictionary and note the definition below.

6. Why did Paul add covetousness to his list? How is covetousness idolatry?

7. What makes idolatry so bad? Read Exodus 20:1-6.

8. Read Matthew 6:19-24. What does Jesus have to say about what we treasure, pursue, or value?

9. Read Matthew 6:19-24. What does Jesus have to say about what we treasure, pursue, or value?

10. Why are we instructed to put to death earthly things? What damage are they doing to us? Can we simply ignore them or turn our attention elsewhere? See Romans 8:13, 1 Corinthians 6:18-20, and Galatians 5:19-21.

11. How should you go about putting to death these earthly appetites? See Matthew 5:27-30 and 1 Thessalonians 1:9-10.

12. Read verse 6 in the KJV. How is it different than the ESV?

13. Disobedience can be literally translated as "the condition of being unpersuadable." [7] The children of disobedience are obstinately opposed to the divine will of God and it is on account of this that the wrath of God is coming. Why is this so?

14. Conclude your study today by reading Job 31:1–12. How did Job go about putting to death that which was earthly in him? Do you think he accomplished what we are instructed to do in Colossians 3:5-6? What steps do you need to take today to kill the earthly things in your heart? Ask the Lord now for His instruction and power to obey.

7 Strong, James. "Disobedience." The New Strong's Expanded Exhaustive Concordance of the Bible Red Letter Edition, Thomas Nelson Publishers, 2001, pp 33.

DAY FOUR

"In these you too once walked, when you were living in
them. But now you must put them all away: anger,
wrath, malice, slander, and obscene talk
from your mouth."
- Colossians 3:7-8

1. Read verses 7 and 8 in the NIV. In verse 7, what does
the word "these" refer to?

2. What does it mean to have walked in these things?
Who were you following when you *walked* this way?
See Ephesians 2:1–2.

3. Look up the words below in a dictionary and note their definitions below.

Anger -

Wrath -

Malice -

Slander -

Obscene Talk -

4. "But now," what has changed? Read Titus 3:3-5.

5. According to Ephesians 4:26-32 and 5:4, what does God desire instead of these earthly things?

6. Read today's Scriptures in the AMP. What word is used instead of put them all away? How do you rid yourself of the practices you were once addicted to?

7. The KJV instructs believers to "put off all these." What imagery does this suggest?

8. Look up Romans 13:12–14 in the AMP. Verse 14 says to "make no provision for indulging the flesh." To make provision means to supply.[8] Have you supplied your flesh with indulgences that are harmful and damaging? Ask the Lord if there are provisions for indulging the flesh in your life that He would like to help you put to death. What are they? What is one practical way you can begin denying your flesh this?

8 "provision." Def. 8. Dictionary.com, 2018.

DAY FIVE

"Do not lie to one another, seeing that you have put off the old self with its practices and have put on the new self, which is being renewed in knowledge after the image of its creator. Here there is not Greek and Jew, circumcised and uncircumcised, barbarian, Scythian, slave, free; but Christ is all, and in all."
- Colossians 3:9-11

1. Paul ends his discourse on putting off earthly things with an instruction to put off lying. Read Genesis 3:1-7. Who told the first lie and what was it?

2. When did God first instruct His people not to lie? To whom was the message given? See Exodus 20:16.

3. According to Jesus, when a person lies, who does he act like or, in the case of unbelievers, belong to? See John 8:44.

4. Look up Psalms 119:163 and Proverbs 13:5. What is the attitude of a righteous person toward falsehood?

5. What is another name for the Holy Spirit? See John 16:13.

6. Is it possible to continue lying even when you have been sealed by the Spirit of Truth? How so? How does this affect the Holy Spirit inside of you?

7. The KJV refers to the old self and new self as the "old man" and "new man." Look back over your studies for this week and fill out the table below with a list of traits for each man or self. What do each walk in?

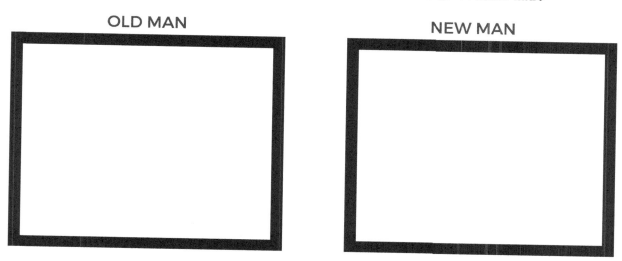

8. What does it mean that the new man is being *renewed in knowledge after the image of its creator*? How does this occur? See Ezekiel 11:19, Romans 8:28–30, and Ephesians 4:22–24.

9. At the beginning of verse 11, Paul uses the word *here*. Where or what is *here*?

10. Verse 11 concludes with a list of distinctions among the people of Paul's day. Look up the Scriptures below and note how they inform your understanding of verse 11.

Isaiah 42:1-4 -

Ezekiel 47:21-23 -

Romans 3:22 -

Romans 10:12 -

1 Corinthians 12:13 -

Galatians 5:6 -

11. Sum up what Paul means by saying *Christ is all, and in all*.

12. Re-read Colossians 3:1-11. Paraphrase the passage in just a few sentences.

13. How is this message relevant to you or your context today?

Put On and Put In

COLOSSIANS 3:12-17

DAY ONE

Video Teaching Notes:

Listen to the entire book of Colossians on www.biblegateway.com or the YouVersion Bible app. Read Colossians 3:12-17 in two or three different translations (ESV, NIV, KJV, AMP).

1. Summarize Paul's central themes in this passage.

2. What excites you or captures your interest in this passage?

3. Are any parts of the passage difficult to understand? What questions do you have about the text?

DAY TWO

"Put on then, as God's chosen ones, holy and beloved,
compassionate hearts, kindness, humility, meekness,
and patience, bearing with one another and, if
one has a complaint against another, forgiving
each other; as the Lord has forgiven you, so
you also must forgive."
- Colossians 3:12-13

1. In last week's Scriptures, Paul instructed you to put off the things associated with your old self. What happens when we put something off, but don't put something else on? What state do we find ourselves in?

2. What is the purpose of clothing or coverings? Make a list of everything clothes or bodily coverings (blankets, shelter) do for us.

3. Chosen means to be "chosen out of a number or selected."[9] Given this definition, how does God Feel about you or view you? See 1 Peter 2:4.

4. Holy means to be "separated from sin and consecrated to God."[10] Given this definition, how does God feel about you or view you? Look back at Colossians 1:22.

9 Strong, James. "Elect." The New Strong's Expanded Exhaustive Concordance of the Bible Red Letter Edition, Thomas Nelson Publishers, 2001, pp 81.

10 Strong, James. "Holy." The New Strong's Expanded Exhaustive Concordance of the Bible Red Letter Edition, Thomas Nelson Publishers, 2001, pp 3.

5. Beloved means "those who are welcomed, entertained, are looked at fondly by another" and "loved dearly."[11] Given this definition, how does God feel about you or view you? The word beloved in the Greek is a derivative of the word agape which Paul uses in Romans 5:8. How does God love us?

6. Why should these three things (being chosen, holy, and beloved) drive us to put on the things of the Lord?

11 "Beloved." Strong's Edition: King James Version, updated ed. StudyLight.org, https://www.studylight.org/interlinear-bible/colossians.

7. Define each thing we should put on. Then look up each Scripture and note how Jesus exemplified for us how each trait or "article of clothing" is to be worn.

Compassionate hearts – Matthew 15:29-39 –

Kindness – Matthew 19:13-14 –

Humility – John 13:1-17 –

Meekness – Isaiah 53:7 and Matthew 4:1-11 –

Patience – Mark 10:35-45 –

8. Look up the verb *to bear* in the dictionary. What does it mean *to bear with one another*?

9. Why do we require an admonition *to bear with one another*? Do we do this naturally?

10. At the end of verse 13, Paul instructs his readers to readily practice forgiveness. How does understanding how *the Lord has forgiven you* better enable you to forgive others?

11. Does Paul list any conditions on his instructions to forgive? Why or why not?

12. Do you find it difficult to forgive those with whom you have quarreled? Do you have a complaint against anyone right now? Ask the Holy Spirit to reveal to you if you are holding anyone in unforgiveness. If you are, take a step of obedience and forgive as the Lord forgave you.

DAY THREE

"And above all these put on love, which binds everything
together in perfect harmony."
- Colossians 3:14

1. Why does Paul begin verse 14 by instructing us to put
on love above all these? Why above the other virtues?

2. Consider an overcoat which you put on above your
regular clothes. What is the purpose of an overcoat and
how does it affect what is underneath it – namely, the
clothes and the body?

3. Given your answer to question 2, how does putting
on love above affect the other virtues within it?

4. What happens when we put on the virtues of the Lord but don't put on love? See 1 Corinthians 13:1-3.

5. Read the rest of 1 Corinthians 13. How is love described?

6. If you always put on love and it looked like the description in 1 Corinthians 13, in what ways would your life look different?

7. How does love act to bind everything together in perfect harmony? Look up 1 Peter 4:8 and note how this Scripture informs your understanding of how love acts as a binding agent.

8. Ultimately, when we put on love, what are we declaring? See John 13:34–35.

9. Take a moment and ask the Holy Spirit to show you how you can put on love today. Record His instructions below and commit, out loud, to obey.

DAY FOUR

"And let the peace of Christ rule in your hearts, to which indeed you were called in one body. And be thankful. Let the word of Christ dwell in you richly, teaching and admonishing one another in all wisdom, singing psalms and hymns and spiritual songs, with thankfulness in your hearts to God."
- Colossians 3:15-16

1. What are one or two themes you see in these verses which have been prevalent throughout the entire book of Colossians?

2. Go to www.studylight.org.
   - Click on Original Language Tools.
   - In the Interlinear Search box, type in "Colossians 3:15" and click Go.
   - Then, change the translation in the search to the King James Version and click Search.
   - Scroll down to the verse and hover your mouse over the word "peace." When it highlights, click on it. The Thayer's/Strong's definitions will then load below the Scripture. Read the definition of "peace" and note it below.
   - What is the *peace of Christ*?

3. What does this peace accomplish for us? See John 14:27 and Philippians 4:6-7.

4. Look up Isaiah 26:3-4. How do we let the peace of Christ rule? What practical steps can you take to remain under the influence of Christ's peace?

5. Go to www.studylight.org.
- Click on Original Language Tools.
- In the Interlinear Search box, type in "Colossians 3:15" and click Go.
- Then, change the translation in the search box to the King James Version and click Search. Scroll down to the verse and hover your mouse over the word "rule." When it highlights, click on it. The Thayer's/Strong's definitions will then load below the Scripture.
- Read the definition of "rule" and note what imagery Paul is using to help you better understand what it looks like to let the peace of Christ rule in your heart.
- How does this affect your understanding of the passage?

6. Why is *letting the peace of Christ rule* a calling to the body? Is it also a calling to the individual? Read Ezekiel 37:26–27.

7. What is the *word of Christ?* Look up John 1:1–18 and describe how this passage informs your understanding of what Paul is encouraging believers to do (let the word of Christ dwell richly). Consider the different possible uses of the word "word."

8. Look up *dwell* in the dictionary and note the definition below.

9. How does it look when *the word dwells richly in a person*? What fruit should you expect to see? Do you see this fruit in your own life?

10. Paul encourages believers to teach and admonish each other in all wisdom. Is this an encouragement for the entirety of the body or just for some (the teachers, pastors, shepherds)? How do you know? What kind of preparation goes into teaching? Can you teach and admonish in all wisdom without adequate preparation?

11. According to the definitions[12] below, what do psalms, hymns, and spiritual songs have in common? How are they complementary?

a. Psalms – A striking or twanging with the fingers of a musical instrument; sacred songs from Scripture sung to musical accompaniment

b. Hymns – Songs of praise addressed to God

c. Spiritual Songs – Songs relating to the human spirit as part of the man which is akin to God and serves as His instrument or organ

12 "Colossians 3:16." Strong's Edition: King James Version, updated ed. StudyLight.org, https://www.studylight.org/interlinear-bible/colossians.

12. What is the relationship between teaching and admonishing in all wisdom and praising or making music to God?

13. Read verse 16 in the KJV. How is it different from the ESV?

14. What does it mean to sing with *grace in your heart*? Have you experienced this? Ask the Holy Spirit to fill you with thanksgiving and gladness. Then turn on some worship music and praise!

DAY FIVE

"And whatever you do, in word or deed, do everything in the name of the Lord Jesus, giving thanks to God the Father through him."
- Colossians 3:17

1. Start today's lesson by paraphrasing verse 17 in your own words.

2. Is there any aspect of your life – word or deed – that isn't covered by this command? If so, what is it?

3. What does *in the name of the Lord Jesus* mean?

4. How do you speak (word) in the name of the Lord Jesus?

5. How do you work (deed) in the name of the Lord Jesus?

6. Look up 2 Chronicles 31:20-21. How is Hezekiah an example of this (doing everything in the name of the Lord)? What can we learn from him?

7. What are the results of doing everything in the name of Jesus Christ? See 1 Peter 4:10-11 for one outcome. What other outcomes are there?

8. How would your life look different if you did everything in the name of the Lord Jesus? Consider your daily agenda, responsibilities, and tasks and make a list of potential differences between how they look now and how they could look if done in the name of the Lord Jesus?

9. Pray and ask the Holy Spirit to reveal one thing to you that you can change so that it is done from now on in the name of Jesus. What is it?

10. Re-read Colossians 3:12–17. Paraphrase the passage in just a few sentences.

11. How is this message relevant to you or your context today?

Households in Christ

COLOSSIANS 3:18-25 AND 4:1

DAY ONE

Video Teaching Notes:

Listen to the entire book of Colossians on www.biblegateway.com or the YouVersion Bible app. Read Colossians 3:18-25 and 4:1 in two or three different translations (ESV, NIV, KJV, AMP).

1. Summarize Paul's central themes in this passage.

2. What excites you or captures your interest in this passage?

3. Are any parts of the passage difficult to understand? What questions do you have about the text?

DAY TWO

"Wives, submit to your husbands, as is fitting in
the Lord. Husbands, love your wives, and do
not be harsh with them."
-Colossians 3:18-19

1. Look up the word *submit* in the dictionary and note
the definition below.

2. In the Greek, the word "submit" was a military word
that denoted ranking or arrangement under.[13] What
does this mean for the marriage relationship?

3. Why are women instructed to submit? How is it
fitting in the Lord? See Ephesians 5:21-24.

13 "Submit." Strong's Edition: King James Version, updated ed. StudyLight.org, https://www.studylight.org/interlinear-bible/colossians.

4. Is this evidence that God loves or prefers men more than women? How do you know? See Galatians 3:26-28.

5. Does this instruction feel unfair to you in any way? Why or why not?

6. According to 1 Peter 3:1-2, what possible blessing can result from a wife's loving submission to her husband?

7. Read Ephesians 5:25-33. What does it mean for husbands to love their wives? How are they instructed to do so in this passage?

8. When both wives and husbands obey their specific mandates to submit and love, what is the outcome? Does it make further obedience to the mandates easier or harder? Why?

9. Read verse 19 in the KJV. How is it different from the ESV?

10. Look up Hebrews 12:14–15. What happens when bitterness takes root in a marriage?

11. Pray and ask the Lord to reveal to you if you have struggled with submission in the past. If you have, repent, and ask Him to empower you to lovingly submit as is fitting in the Lord. Ask the Holy Spirit to speak to you about how He views you when you submit. What does He see in you? Write down whatever He tells you.

DAY THREE

"Children, obey your parents in everything, for this pleases the Lord. Fathers, do not provoke your children, lest they become discouraged."
- Colossians 3:20-21

1. When and where did this command to children originate? Read Exodus 20:12. How is the command in Exodus different from Paul's wording in Colossians. What might account for this difference?

2. According to Ephesians 6:1-3, this command was the first command in God's list of commandments to carry a promise. What is that promise?

3. How might honoring your parents result in long life in God's land? What does that mean for us or how might we understand that promise today?

4. Go to www.studylight.org.

- Click on Original Language Tools.
- In the Interlinear Search box, type in "Colossians 3:20" and click Go.
- Then, change the translation in the search box to the King James Version and click Search.
- Scroll down to the verse and hover your mouse over the word "obey." When it highlights, click on it.
- The Thayer's/Strong's definitions will then load below the Scripture. Read the definition of "obey."
- What does it mean to *obey* and what imagery is referenced in the definition?

5. Are there any conditions in this command? Does the mandate end and if so, when?

6. In what ways can you honor your parents, even as an adult?

7. Look up the word *provoke* and note the definition below.

8. *Discouraged* means "broken in spirit."[14] How might provocation lead to discouragement?

9. What fruit can come of discouragement?

14 "Discouraged." Strong's Edition: King James Version, updated ed. StudyLight.org, https://www.studylight.org/interlinear-bible/colossians.

10. What instructions does Scripture offer for raising our children rightly? Look up the Scriptures below and note what advice or direction is given regarding how we should bring up our children.

Deuteronomy 6:4-9 -

1 Samuel 1:27-28 -

Proverbs 29:17 -

Matthew 19:14 -

Ephesians 6:4 -

11. Pray now and ask the Lord for a specific word of encouragement for your child or children today. What did He say? Be sure to share God's word of encouragement with them.

DAY FOUR

"Bondservants, obey in everything those who are your earthly masters, not by way of eye-service, as people-pleasers, but with sincerity of heart, fearing the Lord. Whatever you do, work heartily, as for the Lord and not for men, knowing that from the Lord you will receive the inheritance as your reward. You are serving the Lord Christ."
- Colossians 3:22-24

1. *Bondservants*, as described in Scripture, are those who were in permanent relationships of servitude in which they had voluntarily given themselves up to the will of another.[15] The condition was different from indentured servanthood in that being a bondservant was a permanent arrangement whereas indentured servants would usually serve for 6 years, and were then set free (Exodus 21:2-6). Can you think of a modern-day equivalent of the bondservant? Who is this message for today?

15 "Servants." Strong's Edition: King James Version, updated ed. StudyLight.org, https://www.studylight.org/interlinear-bible/colossians.

2. What is *eye-service*? What are *people-pleasers* or "menpleasers" (KJV)?

3. Read Matthew 6, verses 1–8 and 16–18. What does this tell you about serving *in order to be seen by others?* What is in store for menpleasers?

4. How does *sincerity of heart* and *fear of the Lord* keep us from serving only as people-pleasers?

5. What changes when you work for the Lord and not for men? Are you ever disappointed? Do you serve differently if you are serving the Lord, not people (NIV)?

6. Verse 24 indicates that you will *receive the inheritance as your reward*. Refer to your study in Week 1: Day 5. Read what you wrote regarding your inheritance and sum it up below. What is your inheritance?

7. Is there anything an earthly master could offer you (money, benefits, fame) that compares to your inheritance in Christ? Why or why not?

8. Do you struggle with people-pleasing? Do you work harder to garner favor when an individual in a position of authority is watching you? Pray now and ask the Lord to search your heart. If He reveals this sin to you, repent, and then ask Him to empower you to *work heartily as for the Lord*.

DAY FIVE

"For the wrongdoer will be paid back for the wrong he has
done, and there is no partiality.... Masters, treat your
bondservants justly and fairly, knowing that you
also have a Master in heaven."
Colossians 3:25 and 4:1

1. What is Paul's purpose in inserting verse 25 in
between the messages of verse 24 and verse 1 of
Chapter 4? What is he trying to communicate?

2. Go to www.studylight.org.
   - Click on Original Language Tools.
   - In the Interlinear Search box, type in "Colossians 3:25"
     and click Go.
   - Then, change the translation in the search box to the
     King James Version and click Search.
   - Scroll down to the verse and hover your mouse over the
     word "persons." When it highlights, click on it.
   - The Thayer's/Strong's definitions will then load below
     the Scripture.
   - Read the definition of partiality, or "respect of persons"
     as it is rendered in the KJV. Who are people naturally
     partial to?

3. Look up 2 Chronicles 19:7 and Job 34:18-19. Why doesn't God show partiality?

4. Read James 2:1-13. How does God regard partiality or "favoritism" (NIV) in His people? How are we to speak and act?

5. How does understanding that you have a Master in Heaven influence you to treat others *justly and fairly?* Read Matthew 18:21-35. How does this passage inform your understanding of Colossians 4:1?

6. Pray and ask the Lord to convict you of any partiality in your relationships with others. Ask Him to give you His eyes to see those who are considered poor in the eyes of the world. What does He see when He gazes upon them?

7. Re-read Colossians 3:18–25 and 4:1. Paraphrase the passage in just a few sentences.

8. How is this message relevant to you or your context today?

Walking in Wisdom Toward Outsiders

COLOSSIANS 4:2-18 AND PHILEMON 1

DAY ONE

Video Teaching Notes:

Listen to the entire book of Colossians on www.biblegateway.com or the YouVersion Bible app. Read Colossians 4:2-18 in two or three different translations (ESV, NIV, KJV, AMP).

1. Summarize Paul's central themes in this passage.

2. What excites you or captures your interest in this passage?

3. Are any parts of the passage difficult to understand? What questions do you have about the text?

DAY TWO

"Continue steadfastly in prayer, being watchful in it
with thanksgiving. At the same time, pray also
for us, that God may open to us a door for
the word, to declare the mystery of Christ,
on account of which I am in prison –
that I may make it clear, which is
how I ought to speak."
- Colossians 4:2-4

1. Read today's Scripture in the AMP. Consider each word below and note what it means for your personal prayer life.

Persistent –

Devoted –

Alert –

Focused –

Attitude of thanksgiving –

2. Go to www.studylight.org.
   - Click on Original Language Tools.
   - In the Interlinear Search box, type in "Colossians 4:2" and click Go.
   - Then, change the translation in the search box to the King James Version and click Search.
   - Scroll down to the verse and hover your mouse over the word "watch."
   - When it highlights, click on it. The Thayer's/Strong's definitions will then load below the Scripture.
   - Read the definition of watch and note it below.

3. Contained within the definition of *watch* is a warning. What is this warning? What might happen if you are not *watchful*?

4. List some ways below of how you can be watchful in prayer.

5. In verses 3 and 4, Paul asks for personal prayer. What specifically does he request?

6. Paul claims that it is on account of declaring the mystery of Christ that He is in prison. What kind of doors could open that give Paul an opportunity to preach? Is he referring to physical doors or something else?

7. Acts 12:1–18 and Acts 16:16–34 are two accounts of God "opening doors" for the Word. Read these two accounts. How are they similar? How are they different?

8. Look up Revelation 3:7-8. On the chart below, describe what it looks like when people open doors and when God opens doors.

PEOPLE OPEN DOORS	GOD OPENS DOORS

9. Read Ephesians 6:18-20. Paul asks not for clarity of speech here, but boldness (or fearlessness in the NIV) in declaring the mystery of the gospel. Why are both – clarity and boldness – important? Can the message go out if you have one but not the other?

10. Is Paul's prayer still relevant to pray today? Spend some time in prayer for missionaries, persecuted brothers and sisters, and disciples around the world. Ask the Lord to give them clear words and boldness, so that they may fearlessly make known the mystery of Christ to a hurting and desperate world.

DAY THREE

"Walk in wisdom toward outsiders, making the best use of the time. Let your speech always be gracious, seasoned with salt, so that you may know how you ought to answer each person."
- Colossians 4:5-6

1. What does it mean to walk in wisdom? How do you do this?

2. Go to www.studylight.org
   - Click on Original Language Tools.
   - In the Interlinear Search box, type in "Colossians 4:5" and click Go.
   - Then, change the translation in the search box to the King James Version and click Search.
   - Scroll down to the verse and hover your mouse over the word "without."
   - When it highlights, click on it. The Thayer's/Strong's definitions will then load below the Scripture.
   - Read the definition *of them that are without* or *outsiders* and note it below. How does this tie verse 5 to the previous verses?

3. What purpose would walking in wisdom serve *toward outsiders*?

4. What is *making the best use of the time*?

5. Go to www.studylight.org.
   - Click on Original Language Tools.
   - In the Interlinear Search box, type in "Colossians 4:5" and click Go.
   - Then, change the translation in the search box to the King James Version and click Search.
   - Scroll down to the verse and hover your mouse over the word "redeeming."
   - When it highlights, click on it. The Thayer's/Strong's definitions will then load below the Scripture.
   - Read the definition of *redeeming* or *making the best use of the time* and note it below. What two examples are given for making the best use of the time?

6. Practically, what does it look like to *redeem* or *buy back* your, or someone else's, time? Does this excite you to think of it this way? Why or why not?

7. Read Ephesians 5:15–16. Why should you *make the best use of the time* or *make the most of every opportunity* (NIV)?

8. What does it mean that *the days are evil*?

9. Have you ever missed an opportunity to redeem the time you shared with an outsider? How did you feel afterward?

10. Pray and ask the Lord to show you one relationship you have with an outsider. How can you redeem the time you have with her or him?

11. In verse 6, why does Paul talk about salt in the context of speech? What properties of salt might he be referring to in his instruction to *season your speech with salt*?

12. Verse 6 appears to presume that people will have questions for believers to answer. What does Paul presume people will ask about? See 1 Peter 3:15.

13. What does graciousness have to do with knowing how to answer people? Look up Ephesians 4:29.

14. Are there areas of your speech that require more graciousness or salt? Ask the Lord to show you how you can speak in such a way that those who listen may be edified.

DAY FOUR

"Tychicus will tell you all about my activities. He is a beloved brother and faithful minister and fellow servant in the Lord. I have sent him to you for this very purpose, that you may know how we are and that he may encourage your hearts, and with him Onesimus, our faithful and beloved brother, who is one of you. They will tell you of everything that has taken place here. Aristarchus my fellow prisoner greets you, and Mark the cousin of Barnabas (concerning whom you have received instructions - if he comes to you, welcome him), and Jesus who is called Justus. These are the only men of the circumcision among my fellow workers for the kingdom of God, and they have been a comfort to me."
- Colossians 4:7-11

1. *Tychicus*, the likely bearer of the letter to the Colossians, is mentioned a few other times in the Bible. Look up the following Scriptures and indicate what you can deduce regarding the character of Tychicus from these brief references. See Acts 20:1-5, Ephesians 6:21-22, 2 Timothy 4:12, and Titus 3:12. What about him made him so useful to Paul? What can we strive to emulate?

2. *Onesimus*, mentioned in verse 9, is the subject of another Pauline letter. Look up Philemon and read the entire epistle. Who is Onesimus?

3. Who is *Philemon*?

4. Summarize the situation as it stood when Paul wrote the letter.

5. What does this letter suggest about the following ideas or principles of the faith?

Forgiveness –

Transformation and restoration –

Living at peace with others –

Appropriate use of authority –

Motivations for righteousness –

Racial or societal divisions for those in Christ –

6. Paul views both Onesimus and Philemon as his spiritual children. Read 3 John 1:4. What is John expressing in this sentiment?

7. Have you ever experienced the joy of seeing your spiritual children walk in the Truth? Describe your pleasure below. If not, pray now and intercede for those whom you have invested in for the sake of the Kingdom - may they walk in the wisdom of the Lord and the knowledge of the Truth.

DAY FIVE

"Epaphras, who is one of you, a servant of Christ Jesus, greets you, always struggling on your behalf in his prayers, that you may stand mature and fully assured in all the will of God. For I bear him witness that he has worked hard for you and for those in Laodicea and in Hierapolis. Luke the beloved physician greets you, as does Demas. Give my greetings to the brothers at Laodicea, and to Nympha and the church in her house. And when this letter has been read among you, have it also read in the church of the Laodiceans; and see that you also read the letter from Laodicea. And say to Archippus, "See that you fulfill the ministry that you have received in the Lord." I, Paul, write this greeting with my own hand. Remember my chains. Grace be with you."
Colossians 4:12-18

1. Look back at Colossians 1:3-7. Who originally brought the message of the gospel to Colossae?

2. Paul describes *Epaphras* as one who struggles, "wrestles" (NIV), or "labors fervently" (KJV) in prayer for the Colossian people. What is the fruit of Epaphras's work?

3. Epaphras likely single-handedly brought the gospel to three different cities – Colossae, Hierapolis, and Laodicea (Colossians 4:13). What does this suggest for one person who is committed to the spread of the Truth and is willing to be used of by God?

4. The city of *Laodicea* is mentioned elsewhere in Scripture in the book of Revelation. Read Revelation 1:9-11 and 3:14-22. Who is the "Amen" - the author of this letter to the Laodiceans?

5. What sins were the Laodiceans guilty of tolerating?

6. What does it mean to be *cold*? What does it mean to be *hot*?

7. What does it mean to be *lukewarm*? Why is this such an affront to God? See Matthew 6:24.

8. What is God's *counsel* to combat this condition?

9. How do we respond and buy gold, white clothes, and "eyesalve" (KJV) from God?

10. Paul concludes his letter to the Colossians with an admonition to *remember his chains*. What purpose does this request serve?

11. Read Hebrews 13:3. Pray and ask the Lord to show you, in what specific way or ways you can continue to *remember those in prison, as though in prison with them*. How can you love and serve your brothers and sisters in chains around the world?

12. Re-read Colossians 4:2-18. Paraphrase the passage in just a few sentences.

13. How is this message relevant to you or your context today?

Final Video Teaching Notes:

Made in the USA
Columbia, SC
11 March 2021